THE
BPMN
GRAPHIC
HANDBOOK

ISBN-13: 978-1512030457
ISBN-10: 1512030457

TABLE
OF
CONTENTS

Chapter ONE

introduction

WHAT IS A PROCESS AND PROCESS MODELING?

Let's define these terms in simple words.

A process is the work someone (or something) do to accomplish an objective.

Process modeling means documenting the current state of a process to describe for example, how it starts, when it's complete, and how a process get from A to B.

THE IMPORTANCE OF PROCESS MODELING

How do you organize to get the work done?

Which are the steps?

Who should do them?

All organizations need to know the answers of these questions in order to **UNDERSTAND** how their business actually works and **IMPROVE** how things are done.

However, until processes are documented, it's impossible to **UNDERSTAND** them, **IMPROVE** them, and **CONTROL** them.

PROCESS MODELING SHOULD BE THE FIRST STEP TO UNDERSTAND AND BEST ORGANIZE THE WAY A BUSINESS WORKS.

MODELS AND COMMUNICATION

So models are a **COMMUNICATION** tool since they help an organization to understand its processes.

Process modeling might be an easy task in a small organization, but think about a large organization:

 An organization with thousands of employees.

 An organization spread across many locations around the world.

 An organization that has relationships and/or dependencies with many suppliers, partners and customers.

It can easily become a mess. Interpretations of the model are hardly the same because people no longer have the same context or the same cultural references, leaving the interpretation of the model to the reader.

Obviously, this is a problem. The elements used to describe business processes must **COMMUNICATE** the **MEANING** intended by the modeler.

And that's where BPMN comes in.

BUSINESS

PROCESS

MODELING

NOTATION

What is BPMN?

The Business Process Modeling Notation provides a **STANDARD** way of representing business processes.

This is done by specifying the sequence of activities that make up the process and its relating information in basically two levels of detail:

Simple

Diagrams with activities, some decisions and important events. If needed, more information can be added, like more specific types of activities and events, roles, etc.

Executable

Diagrams that contain sufficient detail and information that enables the execution of the model by software (Business Process Management Suites).

In some environments, having very detailed models with precise instructions of how the work should happen, allows to use them to drive the work itself by importing them in tools that can execute those instructions.

However, the focus of this book is to show how the Business Process Modeling Notation is used for representing business processes for "high-level" analysis purposes.

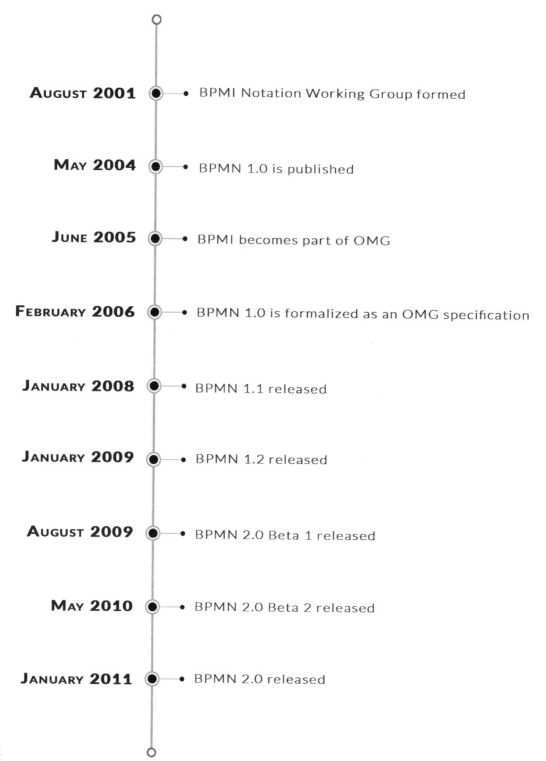

AUGUST **2001** — BPMI Notation Working Group formed

MAY **2004** — BPMN 1.0 is published

JUNE **2005** — BPMI becomes part of OMG

FEBRUARY **2006** — BPMN 1.0 is formalized as an OMG specification

JANUARY **2008** — BPMN 1.1 released

JANUARY **2009** — BPMN 1.2 released

AUGUST **2009** — BPMN 2.0 Beta 1 released

MAY **2010** — BPMN 2.0 Beta 2 released

JANUARY **2011** — BPMN 2.0 released

History of BPMN

In August 2001, 35 organizations formed the BPMI (Business Process Management Institute) Notation Working Group and BPMI.org. Their objective was to create a single notation for process modeling, since at that time, there were many notations and tools for that purpose. They published the first version of BPMN in 2004.

With the growing popularity of BPMN, BPMI.org was acquired by OMG (Object Management Group), home of the popular UML (Unified Modeling Language).

In 2006, the process of formally adopt BMPN as an OMG standard finished. Two years later, a minor update was issued (BPMN 1.1), and a year later, another version with some corrections (BPMN 1.2).

The notation from BPMN 1.2 to BPMN 2.0 didn't change a lot. The two main motivations for BPMN 2.0 were to provide an official interchange format based on XML (eXtensible Markup Language) for process models and to make those models executable in a process engine.

After two *beta* versions, BPMN 2.0 was completed in 2010 and released to the public in January 2011.

MORE ABOUT MODELING

One common mistake is assuming that there's always only **ONE** correct model.

When you make a model, you're always choosing what to include and what to exclude. You may want to show different levels of detail or focus on certain areas, but generally, there's often a tendency to capture more detail than necessary.

For example, consider how to model the scheduling of an appointment for a medical checkup. The first step could be request for the patient information, then check for an available date, and finally, register the appointment. But what if we like to schedule more than one appointment, or if there's no availability, and at the end, should we print or email a confirmation, or both?

BPMN is flexible, meaning it can handle many situations and requirements. So instead of worrying about developing the correct model, you should be worrying about using the notation in a correct way.

> WE ALWAYS NEED TO THINK ABOUT WHO WILL USE THE MODEL AND FOR WHAT PURPOSE.

THERE IS HARDLY EVER ONLY ONE CORRECT MODEL

Chapter ONE

Good BPMN models

To create a good BPMN model, it must be:

Valid
The model should follow the rules of the BPMN specification.

Accurate
The model should reflect the actual process without any erroneous or biased view.

Clear
The model should be unambiguous and easy to understand. It should not depend on any other documentation.

Complete
The model should be as simple as possible, but it should indicate how the process starts, its significant events and its end states.

A good BPMN model **DOES NOT** show:

Why
A process are performed.

When
A process is performed.

How
The steps of a process are
performed.

Chapter ONE

BASIC ELEMENTS AND DIAGRAMS

BPMN uses a set of graphical elements to describe a process. Together, and refined with attributes and properties, these elements create diagrams for organizations of all sizes and domains.

However, there's only four key elements in BPMN:

Activity
The steps to perform a process.

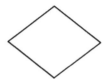

Gateway
Used to control the flow in a process.

Event
Something that happens in a process.

Flow
Used to show the order of the activities of the process.

On a higher level, BPMN allows yo to model four different aspects of business process in four diagrams:

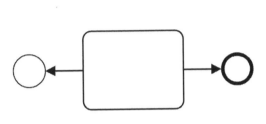

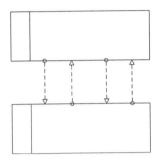

Business Process
Focuses on the activities and events of a process.

Collaboration
Focuses on the sequence of activities, events and messages between participants of a process.

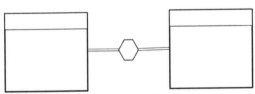

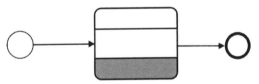

Conversation
Focuses on the message exchange between participants of a process.

Choreography
Focuses on the interactions between participants.

TOKENS

The concept of a token is used to represent the behavior of a model. It's simple, you just imagine a token moving along the diagram, executing the process along its way from start to end.

Let's consider a simple registration process:

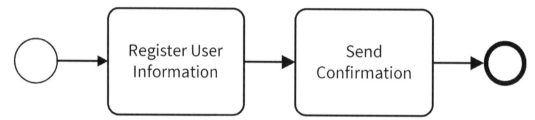

In this example, the start event (represented by the circle at the beginning of the diagram), generates the token:

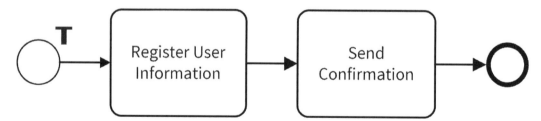

The token then flows to the activity *Register User Information*, causing the activity start:

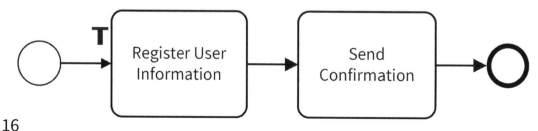

When a token arrives at an activity, the activity starts. This beginning and execution is called an **INSTANCE** of the activity. A new instance is created when a token arrives at an activity.

When the activity finishes its work, it emits a token that travels through the flow to the *Send Confirmation* activity:

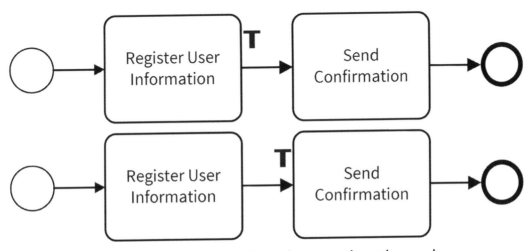

Once the confirmation is sent, the token reaches the end event (represented by the circle at the end of the diagram) and the process completes:

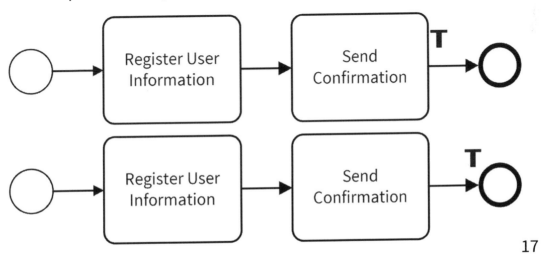

17

Each of the elements in a BPMN diagram handles the flow of a token in an unique, and in some cases, complex way.

With this concept we complete the introduction to BPMN. In the following chapters, we'll focus on the elements and diagrams of the notation.

Chapter TWO

ACTIVITIES

WHAT IS AN ACTIVITY?

An activity represents an unit of work performed. A step inside a process.

It has a defined start and end and generally requires some kind of input to produce an output.

There are two types of activities:

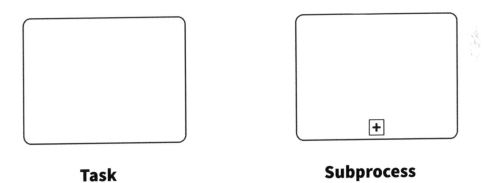

Task   **Subprocess**

THE "+" SIGN INDICATES THAT THE SUBPROCESS CONTAINS MORE DETAIL.

TASK AND SUBPROCESS

A task has no internal parts, it represents a single action.

On the other hand, a subprocess has parts that are modeled in a child-level process, a process with its own activity flow and start and end states.

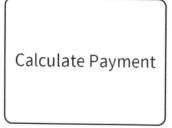

NAME = NOUN + VERB

SUBPROCESSES HAVE OTHER PROCESSES INSIDE

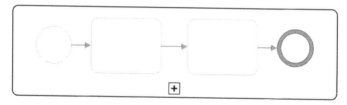

AN ACTIVITY SHOULD BE LABELED AS NOUN-VERB

TASK TYPES

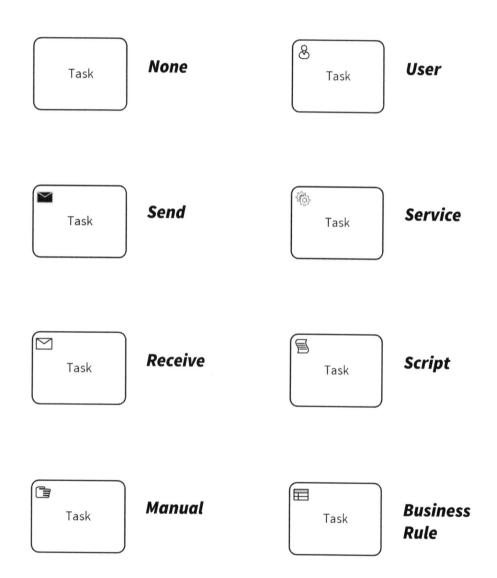

Task types let you represent in a **PRECISE** way how a task should be done.

NONE Task

Task

This is the generic representation of a task and the one you will use more than 90% of the time. All other types are made for advanced uses of BPMN.

SEND TASK

This task represents sending a message to an external participant. Once sent, the task is completed. A message can only be sent between different roles (more on that on later chapters).

RECEIVE TASK

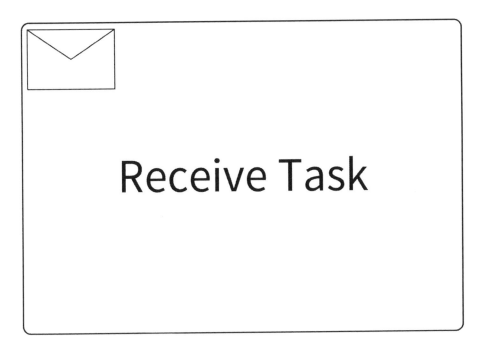

This task waits for the arrival of a message from an external participant. Once received, the task is completed.

Have you notice that the only (graphical) difference with the *Send Task* is the color of the envelop? Keep that in mind, it will be useful later.

MANUAL TASK

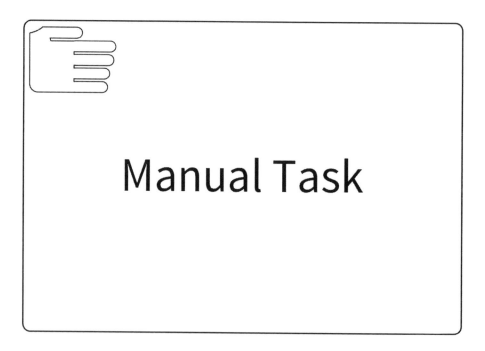

This task represents work that is not automated and is performed outside the control of the BPM engine.

USER Task

This task represents work that is performed by a human user with the help of the BPM engine or another software application.

Chapter TWO

SERVICE TASK

Service Task

This task represents work that is performed by an external system where there is no human intervention, like a web service.

SCRIPT TASK

This task represents work that is performed by the BPM engine as an automated function written in a script language like Javascript.

BUSINESS RULE TASK

This task represents work executed at run-time in a business rule engine, generally, a complex decision.

SUBPROCESSES

Subprocesses can be represented in two ways:

As a **COLLAPSED** subprocess, an activity with a "+" sign indicating that the child-level elements are detailed in a separated diagram.

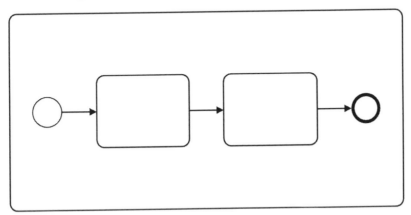

As an **EXPANDED** subprocess, where an activity element encloses the child-level elements.

EXPANDED SUBPROCESSES

There's an important rule about expanded subprocesses:

> AN EXPANDED SUBPROCESS SHOULD HAVE ONE (AND ONLY ONE) START EVENT.

Which means that diagrams like the following are wrong:

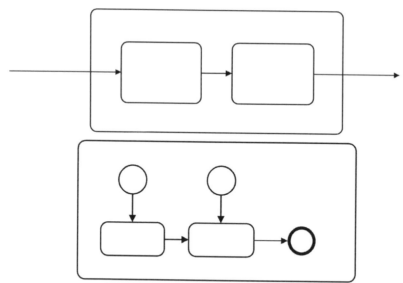

Sequence flows cannot cross the boundary of the subprocess. It must have one start event to indicate the first activity to be executed. In the other case, a subprocess with two start events it's ambiguous. Are they parallel activities? If not, which one is executed first? However, there are exceptions and workarounds which we'll see later.

Subprocess types

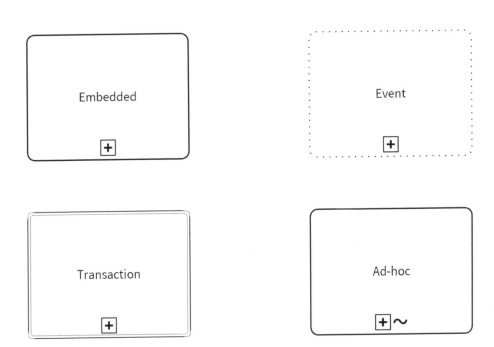

Here, they are shown in their collapsed form.

The embedded subprocess is the normal type of subprocess that we have already covered. It is "embedded" in the parent diagram in either its collapsed or expanded form.

For the rest of the types, the expanded form will be shown in the following pages.

Chapter TWO

EVENT SUBPROCESS

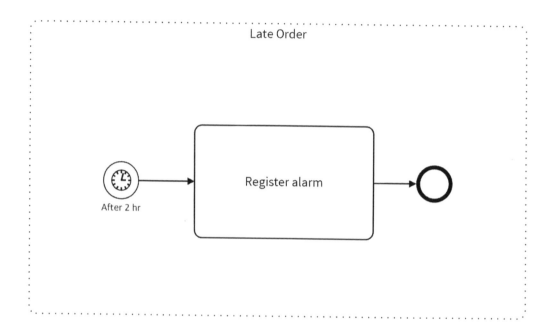

The difference with event subprocesses is that they are not part of the normal flow of the process. Instead, they are triggered by one of the following events:

- Message
- Error
- Escalation
- Compensation
- Conditional
- Signal
- Timer
- Multiple

In the example above, if the parent process takes longer than 2 hours, the event subprocess *Late order* will be trigger. We'll see more about them in the next chapter.

36

TRANSACTION SUBPROCESS

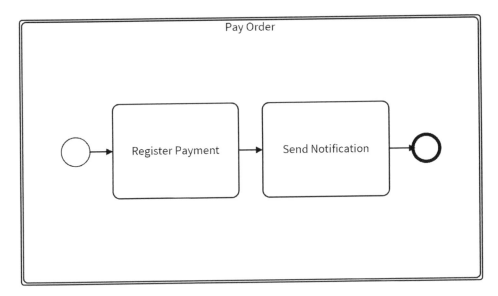

Transaction subprocesses have the following properties:
- **ATOMIC**. Activities inside the transaction are treated as a unit. Either all are performed or none.
- **CONSISTENCY**. The transaction leaves the process (or system) in a valid state.
- **ISOLATION**. The effects of one transaction might not be visible to other parts of the process (or system).
- **DURABILITY**. Once a transaction has finished successfully, changes are persisted permanently.

Transactions have only three possible outcomes (the last two will be reviewed in chapter four):
- Success
- Cancellation
- Exception (error)

AD-HOC SUBPROCESS

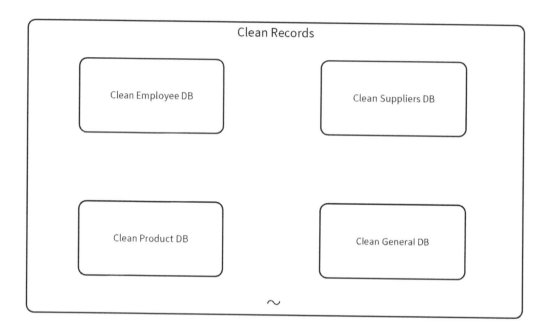

An ad-hoc subprocess is the exception to the rule about required start and end events. In this type of subprocess, the role who performs the process:
- Choose the sequence in which activities are done (they can even be executed in parallel).
- Indicate the activities to do (not every activity is required).
- Indicate when the subprocess is finished.

Because of this, there's no need to have start or end events. Each activity may be performed zero or more times also.

AD-HOC SUBPROCESSES PROVIDE A WAY TO MODEL AN OPTIONAL LIST OF INDEPENDENT TASKS THAT CAN BE SELECTED AND PERFORMED IN ANY ORDER

CALL ACTIVITIES

A call activity is just a reusable activity. It's often compared with a subprocess, and the distinction has to do with the way the child-level detail is used.

If for example, a subprocess is referenced in more than one process (diagram), you can define it in its own diagram and **CALL** it from each process that uses it, instead of copying the same subprocess in every parent process.

Graphically, a call activity has a thick border while a normal activity (task or subprocess) has a thin border.

Just remember, a normal activity has only one parent and it's not available to any other process. A call activity can be included **UNCHANGED**, in many processes (diagrams).

LOOPING

With BPMN you can represent that an activity is executed many times in three ways:

Task ↺	***Standard Loop***

Task ‖‖	***Parallel Multi-Instance***

Task ☰	***Sequential Multi-Instance***

STANDARD LOOP

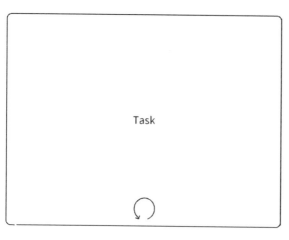

There are two variations:
- **WHILE loop**: First, the loop condition is checked and if it evaluates to true, the activity is performed. Otherwise, the activity is not executed and the process continues (this means there's a chance that the activity will never be performed). Every time the activity finish executing, the condition is evaluated again until it becomes false.
- **UNTIL loop**: First, the activity is performed and then, the loop condition is checked. If it evaluates to true the activity is performed again, if not, the process continues (this means that the activity is performed at least once until the condition is false).

In both cases:
- The looping symbol is the same (the variations are just a property of the activity).
- You can't start an iteration before the previous iteration is finished.
- The number of iterations is unknown (it's determined by the condition).

MULTI-INSTANCE LOOPS

A multi-instance loop is used when a process acts on some kind of collection. In this case the activity is performed once for each item in the collection by an instance of the activity.

This means that the number of iterations will be equal to the number of items in the collection. It is recommended to indicate this with a text label like *For each X*.

If you want the instances to perform in parallel, use three vertical parallel bars.

If you want the instances to perform sequentially, use three horizontal bars.

Just remember, a sequential multi-instance is not the same that a standard loop, being the main difference that the number of iteration are unknown in the latter.

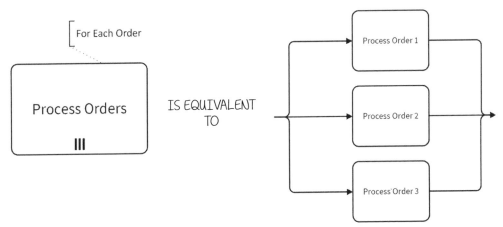

Chapter TWO

Chapter THREE

Events

WHAT IS AN EVENT?

An event is something important to the process from a business perspective that just happens.

Events can be classified by their:
- Trigger
- Behavior
- Type

The event trigger describes why the event is fired. For example, if it is triggered by the reception of a message, by a time condition, etc.

The event behavior has to do with four categories. The first two are about how events can operate:
- **Throwing**: The event waits for a token to throw a trigger as the result of the event. The event's symbol is drawn filled in.
- **Catching**: The event waits for its trigger and then emits a token. The event's symbol is drawn outlined.

Depending on where it is used and its trigger, the event can have an effect on the activity that sent the trigger:
- **Interrupting**: Meaning that the activity terminates and the flow of the process continues from the catching event. The event's symbol is drawn with a solid boundary.
- **Non-interrupting**: Meaning that the activity continues and the flow at the catching event executes in parallel. The event's symbol is drawn with a dashed boundary.

EVENT TYPES

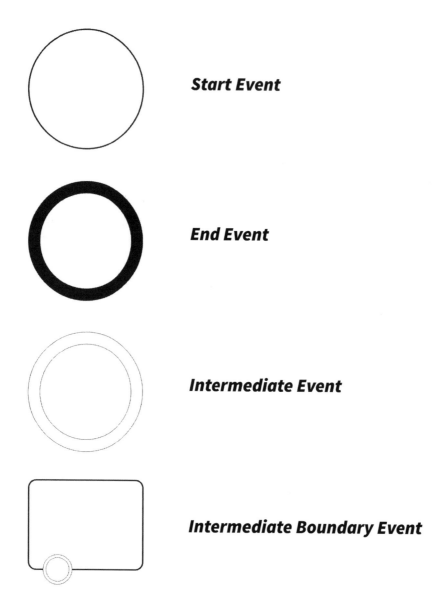

Start Event

End Event

Intermediate Event

Intermediate Boundary Event

START Event

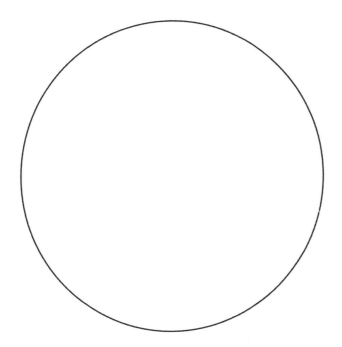

A start event is represented by a circle with a single border. It indicates the start of a process or subprocess.

There are different types of start events that describe the trigger that causes the start of the process.

Start events generate a token when they are triggered. The token then moves down through the event's outgoing sequence flow.

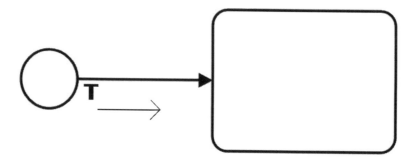

Start events can only have one ongoing sequence flow and they cannot have incoming sequence flows. This rule makes a diagram like the following invalid:

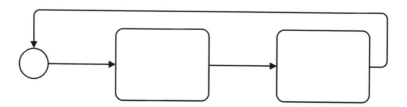

A valid diagram would look like this:

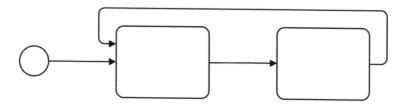

Types of start events

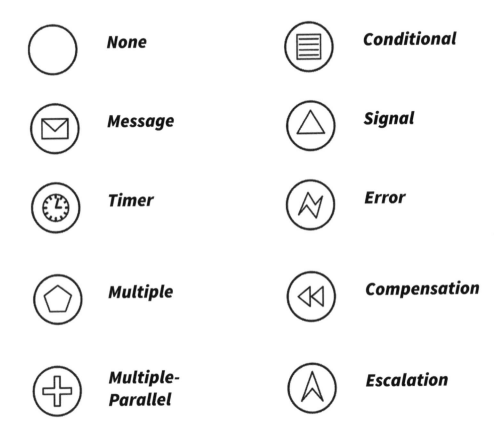

None   Conditional

Message   Signal

Timer   Error

Multiple   Compensation

Multiple-Parallel   Escalation

The error, compensation and escalation types will be covered in the next chapter. The rest will be covered in the following pages.

51

NONE START EVENT

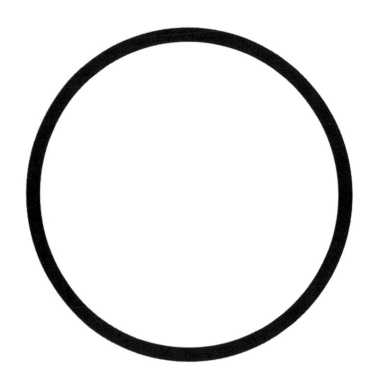

In this case, the trigger (the cause of the event) is not specified, so you use this type of start event when you don't know the cause or it doesn't matter.

This type of start event is also use to mark the start of a subprocess, since a subprocess is not actually started by an event but by a sequence flow.

MESSAGE START EVENT

In this case, the process is started by the reception of a message, which is a form of communication between two business participants. This message is treated as a external request, and the process starts by handling that request.

It's a good practice to label a message start event as *Receive X*, where *X* is the name of the message.

TIMER START EVENT

In this case, the process starts when a specific time condition occurs. This can be a specific date (like July 3, 2010) or a recurring time (every midnight). Each instance represents one of those time events.

It's a good practice to label a timer start event to indicate the time condition.

MULTIPLE AND
MULTIPLE-PARALLEL START EVENT

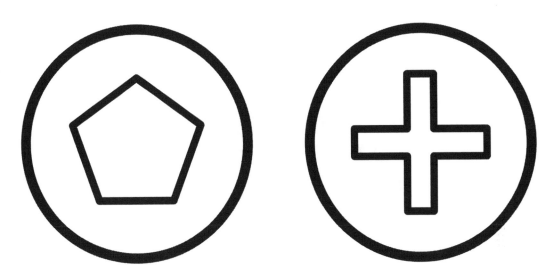

The multiple start event (the one with the pentagon) indicates that a process could be started by any one of the multiple triggers it defines (like a message or a timer). The label should show all the possible trigger conditions.

Each trigger represent an alternative way to start the process. Once triggered, the process will ignore other triggers received.

You should use a multiple start event when all the triggers initiate the same path. Use multiple independent start events when each trigger initiates a different path.

The difference with the multiple-parallel event (the one with the plus sign) is that this requires all triggers to occur to start the process. In the multiple start event, just one trigger (the first) will start the process.

55

CONDITIONAL START EVENT

With this type of start event, the process is started when a condition becomes true.

The condition can be a natural or programming language expression that tests data, like *Order quantity equals 30*.

SIGNAL START EVENT

In this case, the process is started when a signal is received. A signal is defined as a type of communication from a business participant that has no specific target, meaning that all participants can see it and choose to respond it (a message is just sent to one participant).

The label of the event indicates the name of the signal.

EVENT SUBPROCESS
START EVENTS

An event subprocess is one that is triggered by a start event and has no incoming or outgoing sequence flows:

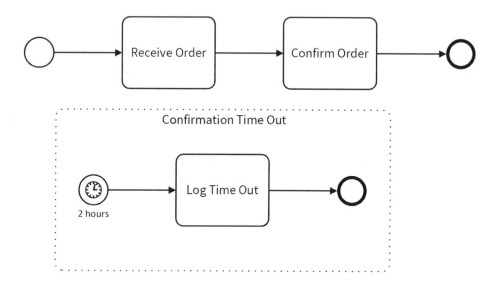

They are also different from other subprocesses because of the dashed boundary.

Start event subprocesses can be interrupting or non-interrupting.

If triggered by an non-interrupting start event (represented by a solid boundary), they run in parallel with the process that contains it. Otherwise, they interrupt that process.

Non-Interrupting start events can have the following types (notice the dashed boundary specific to the non-interrupting type of events):

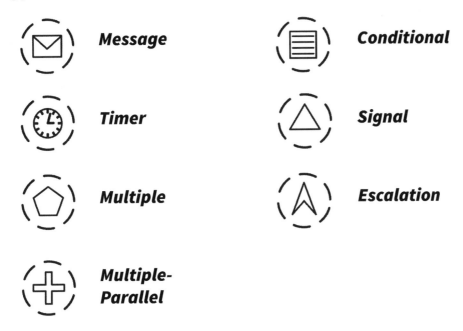

Except for the none start event, the other nine types of start events can be interrupting.

END EVENTS

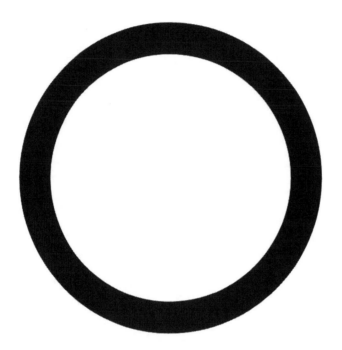

An end event is represented by a circle with a thick border. End events finish a particular path of the process (or the whole process) and generate a result (a message for example).

They just consume tokens, so they have one or more incoming flows but no outgoing flows. Of course, a process can have multiple end events, and it's not complete until all paths have reached an end event.

TYPES OF END EVENTS

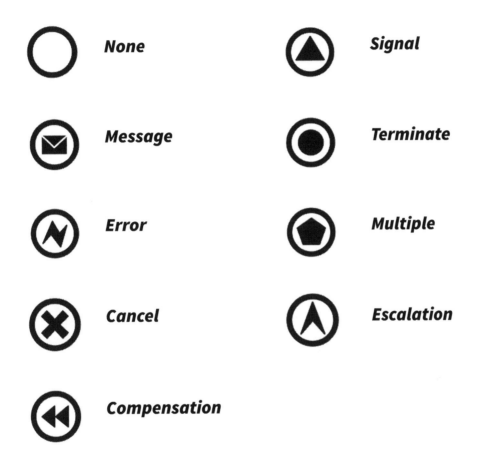

The error, compensation and escalation types will be covered in the next chapter. The rest will be covered in the following pages.

NONE END EVENT

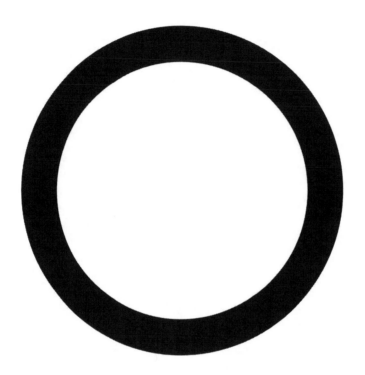

The none end event indicates that there's no result when the process finishes.

If multiple parallel paths end in separate none end events, it's a good practice to merge all into a single none end event, since they don't represent different end states.

MESSAGE END EVENT

A message end events indicates that a message is sent to another participant when the process finishes.

If there are multiple incoming sequence flows from multiple parallel paths to the message end event, the message is sent multiple times.

SIGNAL END EVENT

A signal end events indicates that a process sends a broadcast signal (a signal to all participants) when it finishes.

TERMINATE END EVENT

A terminate end event immediately ends the process or subprocess, even if other paths are active at the time.

If used in a subprocess, this event only ends that subprocess, not the parent process.

MULTIPLE END EVENT

A multiple end event indicates that more than one result is generated when the process finishes.

INTERMEDIATE Events

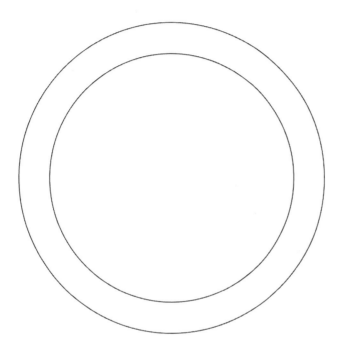

An intermediate event is represented by a circle with a double lined border. It indicates that something happens after the start but before the end of a process.

They can have zero or one input sequence flow and zero or one output sequence flow. For this reason, they may throw or catch depending on their trigger.

So when a token arrives to an intermediate event:

For a *catching* intermediate event, it waits for something to happen (defined by the trigger of the event). Only after receiving that something, it emits a token to the output flow.

For a *throwing* intermediate event, it fires something immediately (defined by the trigger). Then emits a token to the output flow.

Remember that catching events are drawn outlined and throwing events are drawn filled in. So we can say that:

- **START** events are **CATCHING** events since they wait to be triggered. That's why they don't have an infill.
- **END** events are **THROWING** events since they immediately trigger something. That's why they have an infill.
- **INTERMEDIATE** events be **CATCHING OR THROWING** events, depending on the behavior wanted.

Types of intermediate events

CATCH EVENTS   **THROWING EVENTS**

  Message

 Timer

 Error

 Cancel

  Compensation

 Conditional

  Link

  Signal

  Multiple

 Multiple-Parallel

 Escalation

The error, compensation and escalation types will be covered in the next chapter. The message intermediate event (to illustrate how catching and throwing events work together) and the link intermediate event (that doesn't have a start or end event counterparts) will be covered in more detail in the following pages.

The rest of the event types have the same semantics that their start and end events counterparts:

- **TIMER** intermediate event (catch only) waits for time conditions to become true.
- **CONDITIONAL** intermediate event (catch only) waits for a condition to become true.
- **SIGNAL** intermediate event throws or catch a broadcast signal (received by all business participants).
- **MULTIPLE** intermediate event catches any event on its list or throws all the events in the list.
- **PARALLEL-MULTIPLE** (catch only) catches all the events on its list.

In the next page, we see how the sending/receiving of a message is done with intermediate events. Do you remember the Send / Receive tasks on the activities chapter? That's another way to represent it. Remember the color of the icons of those types of task? You must know the reason of those color now.

SENDING/RECEIVING MESSAGES

A *throwing* message intermediate event is used to send messages. When a token arrives at the event, immediately sends a message to a participant.

And then, the token moves to the outgoing sequence flow to continue the process.

On the other hand, a *catching* message intermediate event waits for a message to arrive.

When the message arrives, the event triggers and the token immediately moves to the outgoing sequence flow to continue the process.

Note that if the message arrives before the catching message intermediate event is waiting, the message will be ignored. This situation can cause that the catching event waits indefinitely until another message is sent.

LINK EVENTS

Link intermediate events (also known as just Link Events) are used as page connectors and "go-to" objects.

They are always used in pairs, as a *source* link (*throwing* event) and *target* link (*catching* event) and both must have the same label.

When a token arrives at a source link, the event is triggered and the token jumps to the target link immediately.

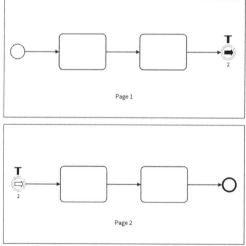

There's always one target link, but there may be many source links. Just remember that they must have the same label as the target link.

BOUNDARY EVENTS

Intermediate events are either placed between activities or attached to the boundary of an activity. The last ones are called boundary events.

Boundary events are catching only (so they are not filled in) intermediate events that may or may not be interrupting to the activity. Events thrown inside an activity are passed up the process hierarchy until some activity catches them.

A common use of boundary events are deadlines or time outs. For example, in:

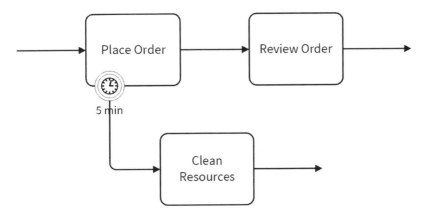

The timer starts at the same time that the activity *Place Order*. If the timer goes off before the activity finishes, this is interrupted and the process continues down the timer's outgoing sequence flow (*Clean Resources* activity). Otherwise, the process continues normally (*Review Order* activity).

TYPES OF BOUNDARY EVENTS

INTERRUPTING	NON INTERRUPTING	
		Message
		Timer
		Error
		Cancel
		Compensation
		Conditional
		Escalation
		Signal
		Multiple
		Multiple-Parallel

Chapter FOUR

Advanced Events

ERROR-RELATED EVENTS

There are four events that are very related and that, their start, intermediate and end types, work together with their catch and throw versions:

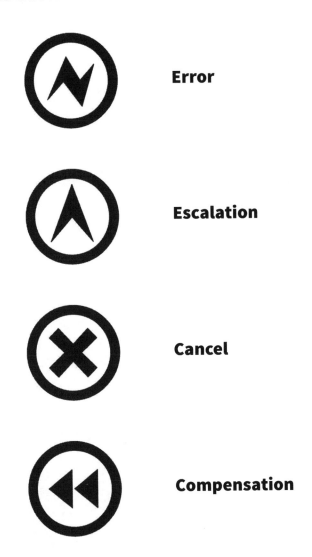

Error

Escalation

Cancel

Compensation

ERROR EVENT

When there's a critical problem in an activity, an error is generated and all work will stop. Because of that, errors events are only interrupting.

To handle an error, we need a throw/catch pair:
1. If the error is somehow expected (it's a known error, generated under certain conditions), throw the error with an error end event to end the activity in which it occurred.
2. You can catch the error at two levels:
    *   At the same process level with an error start event.
    *   With an error boundary event attached to the task or subprocess that generates it.
3. The catching event emits a token to an activity that handles the error.

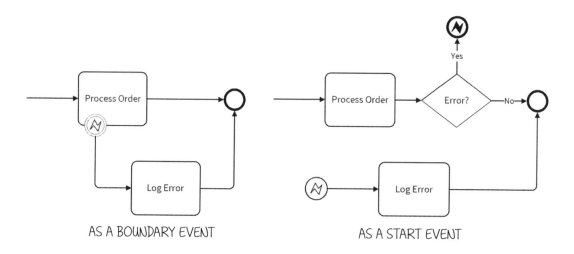

AS A BOUNDARY EVENT   AS A START EVENT

ESCALATION EVENT

Escalations and errors are similar, they're both a deviation from the normal process and they both work in throw/catch pairs, but you can think of escalation as a non-interrupting kind of error that happens inside an activity.

An escalation event is commonly used as a boundary event and in cases where the performer of a task wants to initiate a parallel path of action in the middle of an activity. A good example is asking for support:

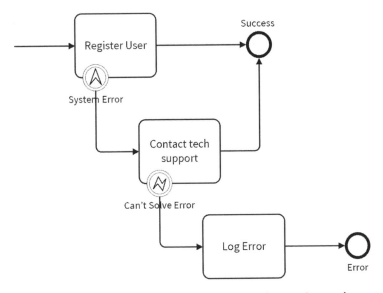

If a system error comes up during a user registration, the operator may contact tech support to try to solve the problem. Only if the error persists, an event error is thrown. This way, the escalation event implies that an error **MAY** be thrown, not that it **WILL** be thrown.

CANCEL EVENT

Another type of error event is the cancel event. It works in throw/catch pairs and it's also interrupting.

The difference is that cancel events are only used with transactional subprocesses (within a transactional subprocess or within a child-level subprocess of it).

There's also a little difference in the meaning. Since it works in the context of a transaction, the cancel event implies that the transaction is rolled-back and may result in (or execute) the compensation of some activities of the transaction.

It has the following semantics:
- The intermediate cancel event can only be attached to the boundary of a transaction subprocess.
- It can be triggered by a cancel end event within the subprocess.

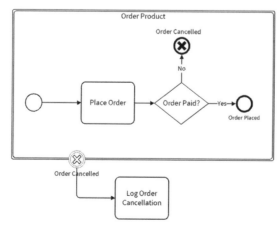

COMPENSATION EVENT

Simply put, compensation means undoing changes.

The compensation mechanism is as follows:
1. Using a gateway, detect the need for compensation.
2. Throw a compensation event, either by using a compensation end event or a compensation throwing event.
3. Roll back completed activities (undoing changes in case the activity made changes). If one activity have a compensation boundary event, the event is triggered.
4. Execute the associated compensation handler.

A compensation handler is a special activity that undo the effect of the activity with which is associated and it can have the form of an event subprocess (if a compensation start event is used) or an activity associated via a catching compensation boundary event.

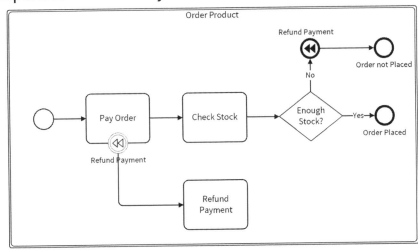

In summary, the semantics of a compensation event are:
- As a start event, compensation is an event subprocess.
- As an end event, compensation is only a throwing event.
- As an intermediate event, compensation is a throwing event used in the normal flow, and as a catching event, it's used only as a boundary event.

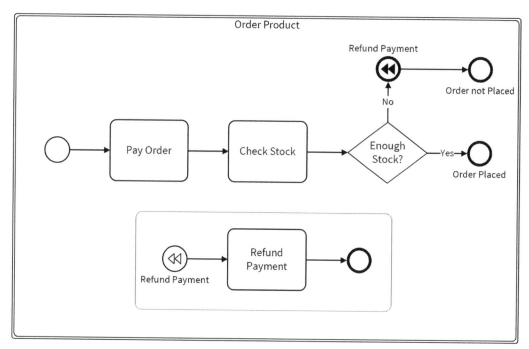

COMPENSATION HANDLER AS AN EVENT SUBPROCESS

Gateways

WHAT IS A GATEWAY?

Gateways are objects that control the flow of the process instead of actually performing something. For example, if you want to include alternative paths depending of the output of something, you use a gateway.

Gateways have two behaviors:
- Converging, that refers what they do to the incoming flows.
- Diverging, what they do to the outgoing flows.

There are five types of gateway, but they are all represented by a diamond:

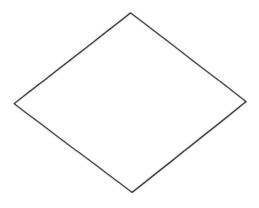

Gateway Types

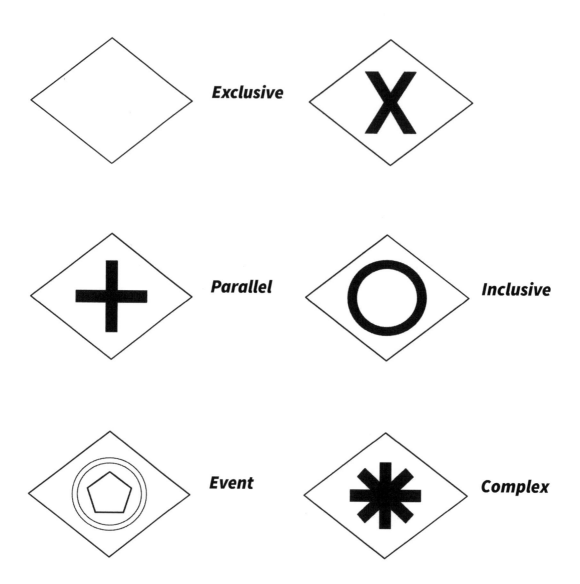

Exclusive

Parallel

Inclusive

Event

Complex

IMPORTANT NOTES

Since gateways have income and outcome behaviors, the types must match, meaning that a gateway cannot be for example, exclusive on the input side, and inclusive on the output side.

Some people think about a BPMN gateway as the same as a decision box in a flowchart, however, it's not. A gateway doesn't make a decision, it just tests a condition. This is an important difference.

For example, to approve or reject something in BPMN, you need a task to do that and then, a gateway that can test the output of the task and route the flow according to the result.

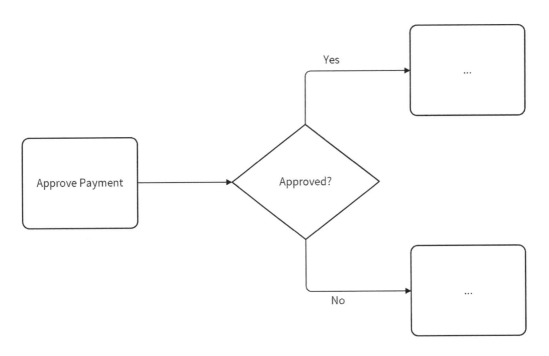

EXCLUSIVE Gateway

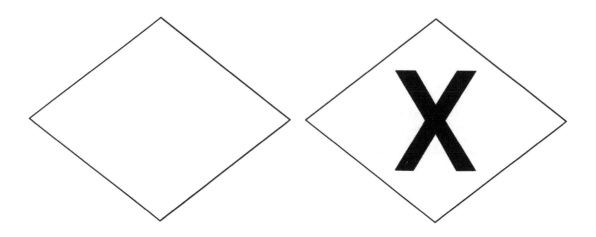

The two shapes above represent an exclusive gateway. There is no difference in meaning between them, but it's a good practice to choose one and use it consistently.

EXCLUSIVE means that the flow of the process (a token) will continue for only one of the gateway's outgoing sequence flows (also known as gates), even when there are multiple of them.

When a token arrives at an exclusive gateway, the conditions on its outgoing paths are evaluated. One of those conditions must evaluate to true. This is required. If none of the conditions are true, the process will be stuck at the gateway.

One way to ensure that the process doesn't get stuck at

an exclusive gateway is to use a **DEFAULT CONDITION** as one of the outgoing sequence flows. A default condition is represented by a sequence flow arrow crossed by a line in this way:

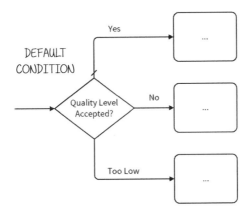

A good practice is to use an exclusive gateway to merge two or more paths. When a token arrives to the gateway, it's immediately moved to the outgoing sequence flow.

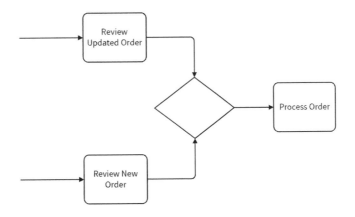

PARALLEL GATEWAY

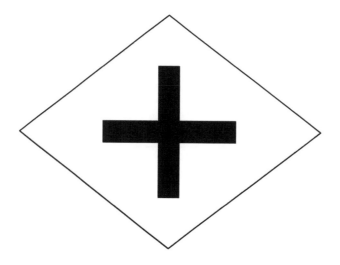

In a parallel gateway, all of its outgoing sequence flows are executed in parallel:

- First, the parallel gateway emits a token on all of its output paths unconditionally.
- Then, all the paths are executed in parallel.
- At the end, the gateway waits for all the tokens from all its paths. This synchronizes the multiple flows into one.

Contrast this behavior against the exclusive gateway's. The exclusive gateway waits for just **ONE** token from any of its paths. The parallel gateway waits for tokens from **ALL** of its paths.

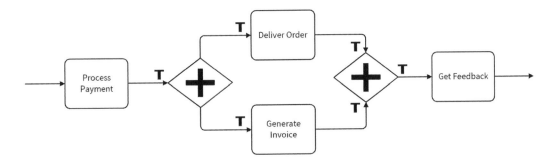

The parallel gateway at the end will wait for all the tokens. When the first token arrives, it is held at the gateway and the flow does not continue. This holding would go on until the last token arrives.

When all tokens have arrived, they are merged and just one token moves down to the outgoing sequence flow.

When the number of parallel sequence flows doesn't match the number of tokens arriving at the end, the process will get stuck, waiting for a token that will never arrive. This is especially true in complex flows for example, when there's more than one gateway used.

ALWAYS MATCH MERGING AND SPLITTING FLOWS IN A PARALLEL GATEWAY.

WRONG

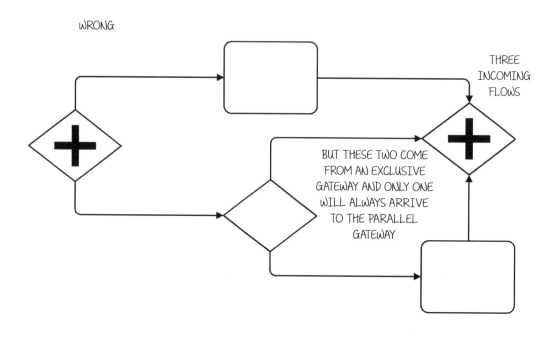

THREE INCOMING FLOWS

BUT THESE TWO COME FROM AN EXCLUSIVE GATEWAY AND ONLY ONE WILL ALWAYS ARRIVE TO THE PARALLEL GATEWAY

RIGHT

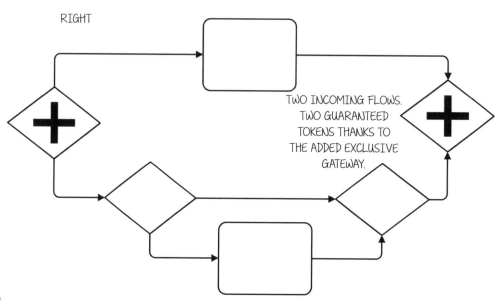

TWO INCOMING FLOWS. TWO GUARANTEED TOKENS THANKS TO THE ADDED EXCLUSIVE GATEWAY.

PARALLELISM

We have three ways to model parallelism (concurrency):

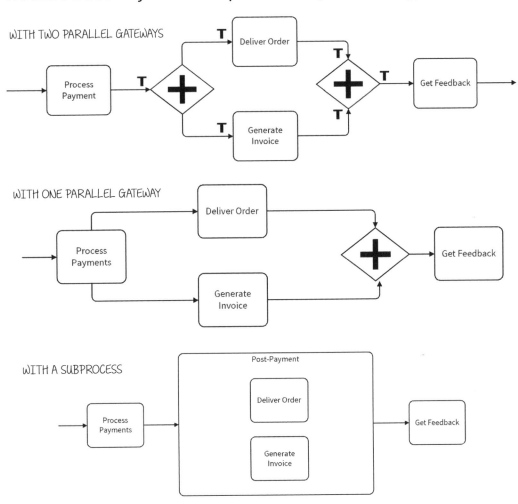

However, the subprocess way should not be considered for the sole purpose of model parallelism. The subprocess must make sense or have business value. Otherwise, is not entirely correct to use it.

EVENT GATEWAY

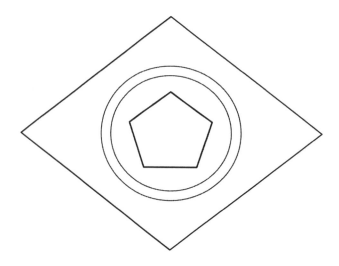

In an event gateway, the decision is based on two or more events that might occur. Because of this, the symbol inside the diamond is the same as the Multiple Intermediate Event.

This gateway also represents an exclusive choice (only one gate is chosen). The chosen path is the event that occurs first. The events are different types of catch intermediate events.

When the token arrives to the gateway, it will split up, sending one token to each of the gateway's events. Since these are catching intermediate events, the tokens will wait until one of them is triggered.

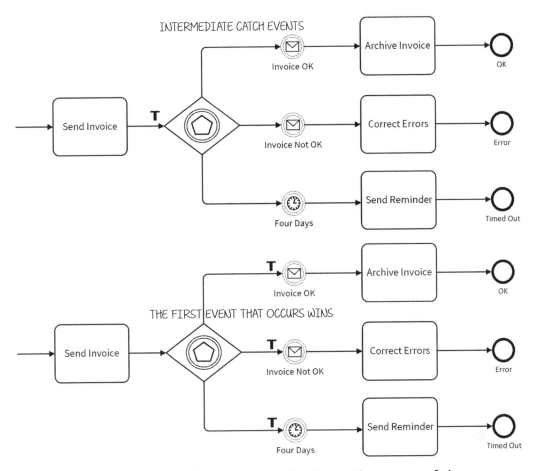

Notice there's three end events that indicate the state of the process when is finished. You should only have one end event if the different flows leave the process in the same state.

Of course, there's the risk that none of the gateway's events may occur. In that case, the process will be stuck at the gateway. The solution (and a good practice) is to always use a **TIMER EVENT** as one of the events for the gateway.

INCLUSIVE GATEWAY

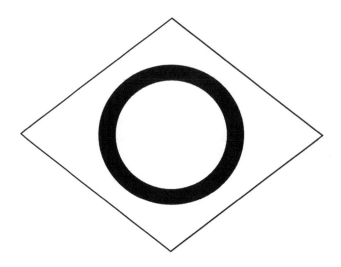

With an include gateway, each path has a condition but more than one could be true. Every true condition will move the token through that sequence flow. If two or more are true, they run in parallel.

That way:
- An inclusive gateway activates **ONE or MORE** paths.
- An exclusive gateway activates just **ONE** path.
- A parallel gateway activates **ALL** paths.

If none of the conditions are true, the process can get stuck. To avoid it, you use a default condition for one of the outgoing sequence flows. This will always evaluate to true if the rest are false (like an *otherwise*).

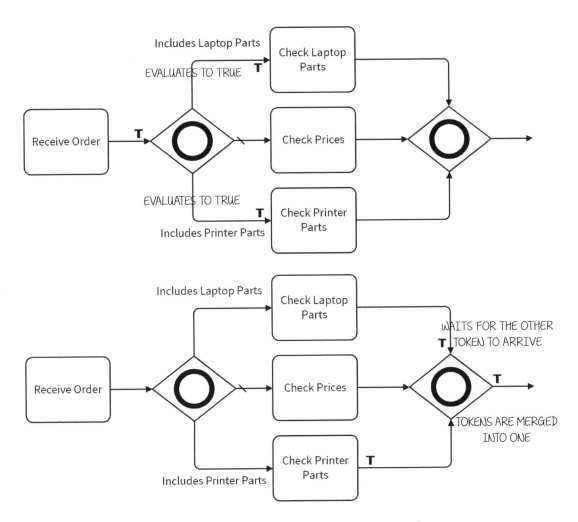

The gateway at the end will determine how many tokens are expected. This way, the gateway will host the first tokens until the last one arrives.

For this reason, it's a good practice to use inclusive gateways in pairs, so the number of incoming and outgoing flows can match.

CONDITIONAL SEQUENCE FLOWS

You can replace an inclusive gateway with conditional sequence flows, that only move down the token when their condition evaluates to true. Here's the previous example adapted to use conditional sequence flows:

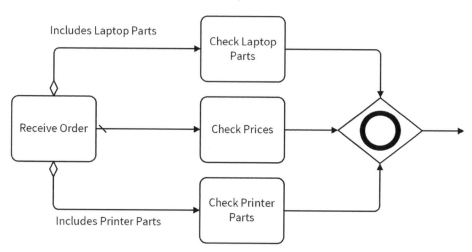

We don't place a gateway at the beginning but two sequence flows with a diamond. They indicate that the flow is only enabled when the condition is true. This notation is only allowed for sequence flows that go out of an activity.

This is just a matter of style. The only recommendation is to use one notation, not both.

Use conditional sequence flows only to replace an inclusive gateway (with conditionally parallel choices). For exclusive choices (where only one path is chosen), it's better to use an exclusive gateway.

COMPLEX GATEWAY

Complex gateways are used in situations where the other types of gateways don't provide support for the desired behavior.

With a complex gateway, you provide your own expression to determine its behavior. For this reason, they are also used to replace a set of gateways by combining them into a single one.

Since the actual behavior will vary each time you use a complex gateway, it must be supported by a text annotation to describe it, like in the following example:

99

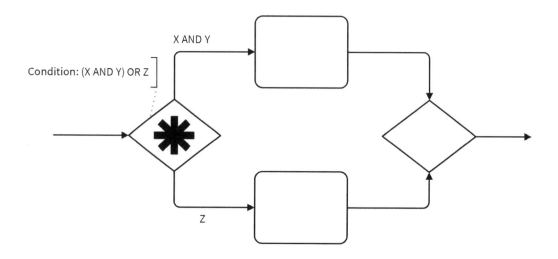

A complex gateway is often use with the discriminator pattern. In this pattern there are two or more parallel activities. When one of them finishes (it doesn't matter which), another activity begins. When the remaining activities finish, this another activity won't start again.

For example, an assessment can start with the output of either the technical review or the business review, whichever finishes first. If we had another type of gateway or no gateway at all, the assessment task would be triggered twice.

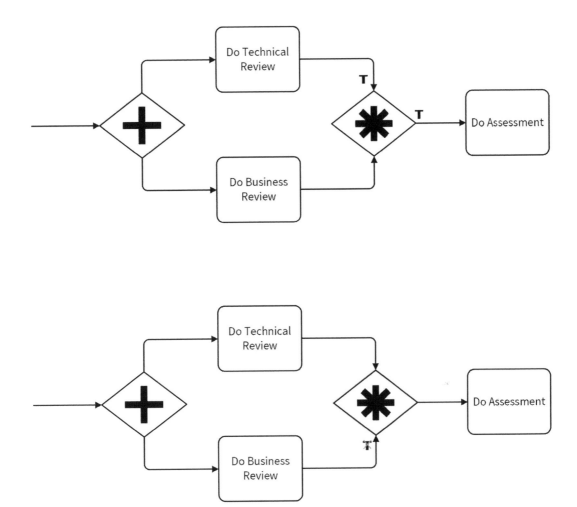

Chapter FIVE

Chapter SIX

Artifacts
and
Data Objects

WHAT IS AN ARTIFACT?

Artifacts give us a way to provide additional information about a process, specifically, the data involved.

There are two types of artifacts:

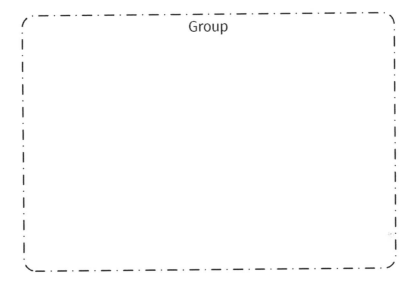

GROUPS

A group is just a dashed round rectangle that encloses a set of objects in order to tag them or highlight them.

They don't impose any constraints or rules (for example, sequence flows cross them like they weren't there). They are just a graphical feature of BPMN.

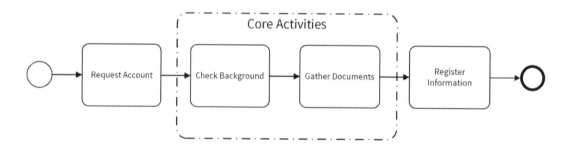

Don't make the mistake of treating a group like a subproccess either. You can't attach an event to the boundary of the group, nor it defines a child-level in the process. It just a graphical way to tag o highlight a set of elements.

TEXT ANNOTATIONS

Text annotations provide a way to add information or notes about a process or its elements to a diagram.

They can be placed anywhere on the diagram and they can be attached to any element as well.

A text annotation is a open text box that uses a line (called association) to connect to an element.

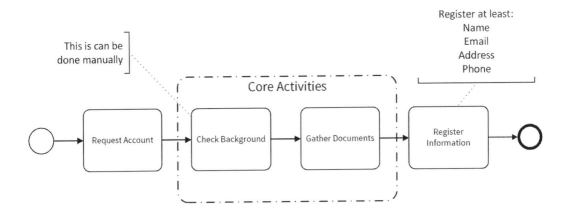

Just like groups, text annotations don't affect in any way the process.

WHAT IS A DATA OBJECT?

In early versions of BPMN, data objects belonged to the artifacts group, but in BPMN 2.0, data objects are recognized as first-class elements.

A data objects can model the inputs and/or outputs of an activity like an invoice or receipt. Generally, they represent documents, but in theory, they can represent any kind of data.

Data objects are represented by a rectangle with a dog-ear.

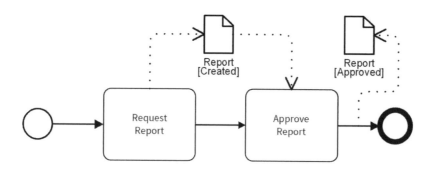

Data objects are connected by a dashed arrow (also called data association) to other elements. This doesn't affect the flow of the process, it just shows the input/output of an activity.

Data objects can also have states that show how the object is updated by the activities of the process. This state is shown under the name of the data object between brackets.

108

Data objects types

There are four types of data objects. The first three can also represent a collection of objects. Since there is not much to know about data objects, they won't be covered in more depth.

 Generic data objects are used to show how data flows within a process.

Data Object — Collection of Data Objects

  Used when the data object represents an input to an activity.

Data Input — Collection of Data Inputs

  Used when the data object represents an output to an activity.

Data Output — Collection of Data Outputs

 This data object represents an external data store such a database that store or provide data.

Data Store

Chapter SIX

Chapter SEVEN

Swimlanes
and
Collaboration
Diagrams

SWIMLANES

When you want to organize or partition activities in a diagram, swimlanes are the solution. There are two types:

- Pools. Each pool represents a participant in the process.

- Lanes. Lanes provide a way to partition a pool based on the characteristics of the process or its elements.

Pool	Lane	
	Lane	

Pools

A pool represents **ONE** participant of a business process.

Participants can be business roles or entities, like a customer, a buyer, a supplier, support team, etc.

Pools are represented by a rectangle that acts as a container of other BPMN elements.

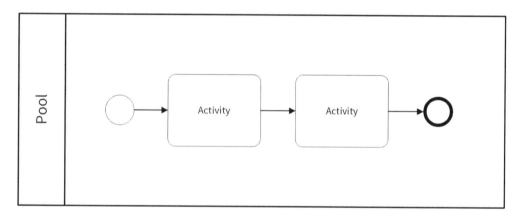

But pools are not required to contain elements. Pools that don't show elements within are called *black-box* pools.

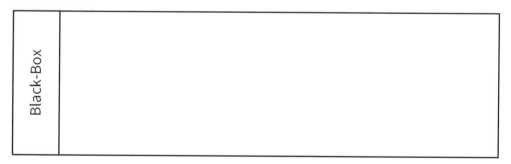

USE A BLACK-BOX POOL TO REPRESENT AN EXTERNAL ENTITY OR SERVICE

A good practice is to use a black-box pool to represent an external service or entity. Some common examples are the customer or a system.

One common mistake people do is to put activities and other elements in a customer or another external entity pool.

Do your really know the internal processes of your customer? Most of the time the answer is no, that's why is a mistake. You can exchange messages like confirmations, notices of failure, etc., but you cannot know all the internal steps of the side of its process. That's the reason to use a black-box pool.

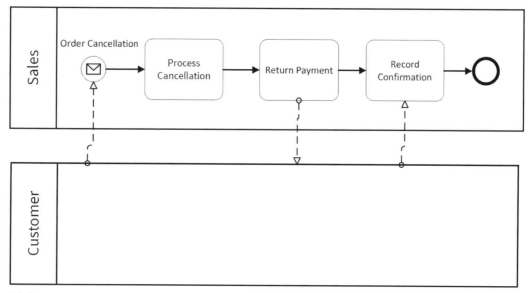

MESSAGE FLOWS

Sequence flows represent the normal flow of a process, but between pools, the communication is done through message flows (dashed arrow lines):

Message flows depict a transfer of information and generally, the actual messages or their content are not shown, so they just display an indication that the messages are sent.

A message flow connects elements inside pools, but when working with black-box pools, message flows connect to its boundary.

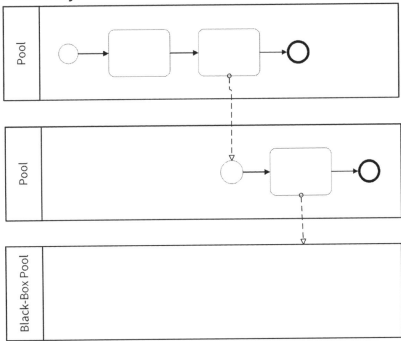

Message flows are subject to these two rules:
- Message flows are only used between participants. This means you can't use them inside a pool (use sequence flows instead).

- Message flows don't begin with start events or finish at end events. Think about it, they need to do something in order to initiate or receive a message.

A process initiated by a request for something should be represented by a message start event received from another pool with a message flow. This is a common scenario when modeling processes where a customer is involved.

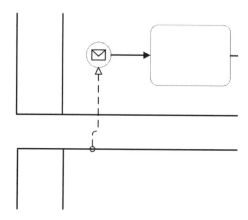

LANES

With lanes you can organize or group related activities inside of a pool. Lanes create partitions inside a pool in this way:

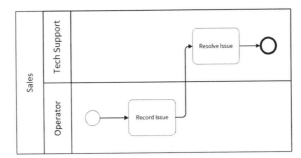

Lanes generally represent organization roles (like manager, agent, etc.), but in theory, they can represent any classification (like products, systems, location, etc.).

The rules to work with lanes are:
- Message flows can't be used inside lanes, just sequence flows.
- Sequence flows can cross lanes
- Lanes can be nested

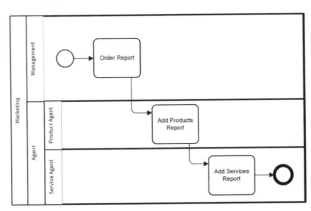

119

CONGRATULATIONS!

NOW YOU ALSO KNOW THE ELEMENTS TO CREATE A COLLABORATION DIAGRAM

COLLABORATION DIAGRAMS

The sole purpose of a collaboration diagram is to show the high level interaction (message flows) between participants. In other words, to show how they **COLLABORATE** together.

So most of the time (although not a requirement), a collaboration diagram is formed by black-box pools.

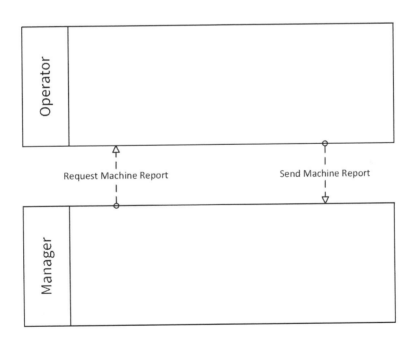

Chapter SEVEN

Conversation Diagrams

WHAT IS A CONVERSATION?

A conversation groups interactions (represented by message flows) between two or more participants that work together to achieve a common goal.

Conversation diagrams model that interaction (the conversation) without any other logic.

Take for example this simple collaboration:

When we group this interaction into a conversation, this is how it looks like:

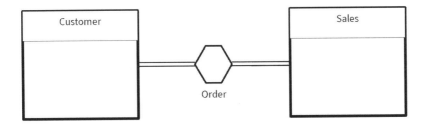

Types of conversation diagrams

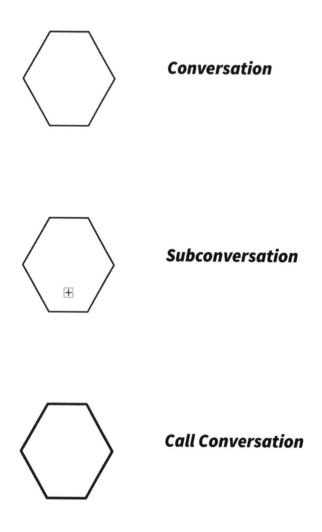

Conversation

Subconversation

Call Conversation

THE CONVERSATION DIAGRAM

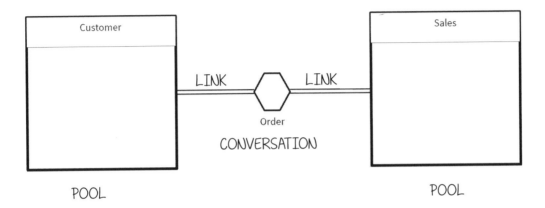

Participants are represented as collapsed pools.

The conversation link represents two or more message flows, so it can represent a complex set of flows in a simple way.

A set of participants of the same kind is represented with the following symbol:

SUBCONVERSATIONS

Just like processes can be broken into subprocesses, we can break a conversation into a subconversation to simplify things.

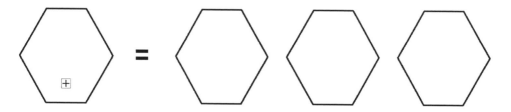

You can use subconversations to start modeling at a high level and then refine the model by adding more detail. Or viceversa, to provide a high level view of a detailed model.

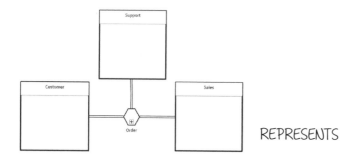

REPRESENTS

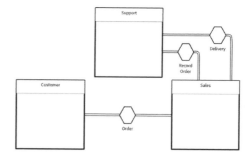

CALL CONVERSATION

A call conversations allow you to **REUSE** (call) an existing collaboration. They use what are known as global conversations, since they can be called in any part of the model as they contain generic pools and message flows just to be reused.

There's also call subconversations (like the example below) that contain nested conversations.

These two forms are drawn with a thick border to differentiate them from the other types of conversations.

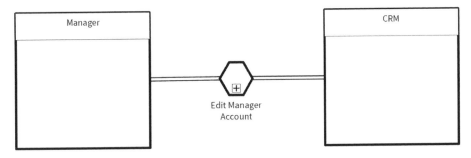

CALLS THE FOLLOWING GLOBAL CONVERSATION

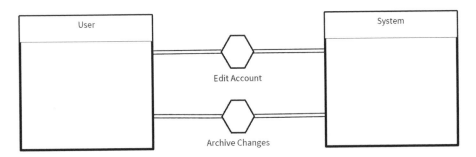

129

Chapter EIGHT

Chapter NINE

Choreography Diagrams

WHAT IS A CHOREOGRAPHY?

A choreography defines the sequence of interactions between two or more participants and it can include elements like gateways and sequence flows.

Take for example this simple collaboration:

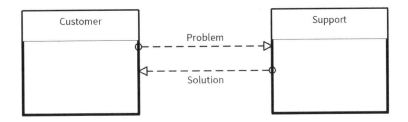

When we express it as a choreography, it looks like this:

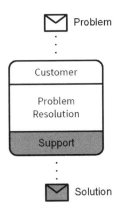

TYPES OF CHOREOGRAPHY DIAGRAMS

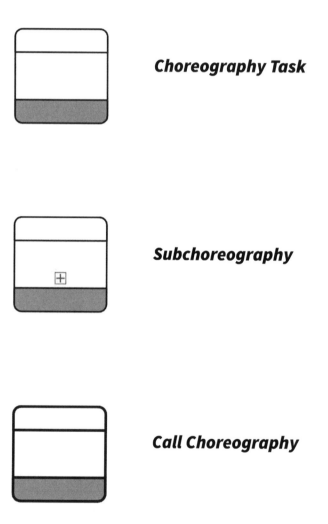

Choreography Task

Subchoreography

Call Choreography

CHOREOGRAPHY TASKS

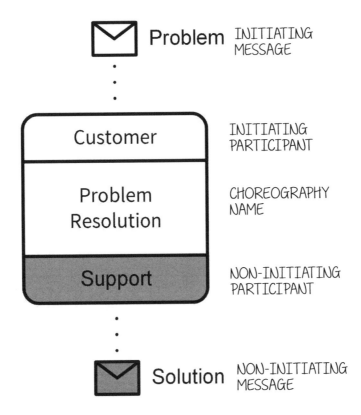

Participants are placed at the top and bottom of the choreography task. The participant that sends the first message is known as the initiating participant. All other participants (there can be more than one) are non-initiating participants and they must be drawn with a shade.

Optionally, the messages sent can be associated with each participant (have you noticed that the non-initiating message is also shaded? This is because it's a response message).

Subchoreographies

Just like processes can be broken into subprocesses and conversations into subconversations, we can break a choreography into subchoreography to simplify things. It can be collapsed or expanded.

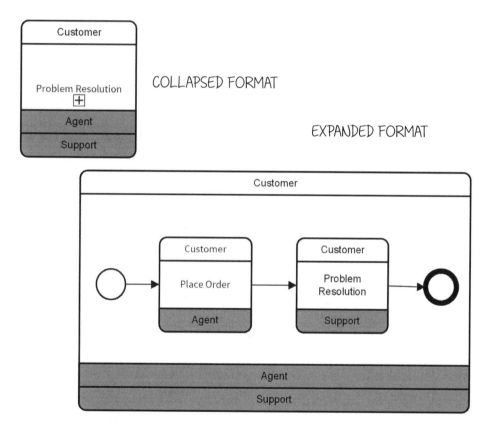

COLLAPSED FORMAT

EXPANDED FORMAT

Notice how all the participant that interact in the lower-level choreographies are listed in the top-level choreography, and how there are start and end events and sequence flows in choreography diagrams.

CALL CHOREOGRAPHIES

Just as there are call conversations, there are call choreographies. They also allow you to **REUSE** (call) an existing choreography using global choreographies.

There's also Call Subchoreographies that contain nested choreographies.

These two forms are drawn with a thick border to differentiate them from the other types of choreographies.

GATEWAYS IN CHOREOGRAPHIES

Choreographies let you express something complex in a simple way. That is the case when using gateways, since branches are not about a single participant but many, so they can represent complex semantics.

The five types of gateways (exclusive, inclusive, parallel, event and complex) can be used in choreographies. The only restriction is that the condition of the gateway can only refer to data exchanged in previous messages. Otherwise, the choreography could not access the data.

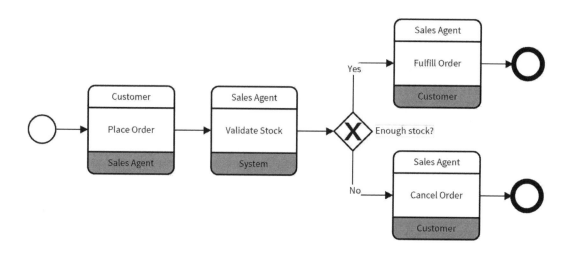

Chapter TEN

how to model
with
BPMN

TOP-DOWN MODELING

Knowing all the elements of BPMN doesn't guarantee the creating of good, meaningful diagrams. You also need a modeling method. The **TOP-DOWN** modeling method is the most recommended one.

Top-down modeling begins with a general agreement among the stakeholders on the scope of the process:

- Where does the process start?
- Where does the process end?
- When does the process is completed?

The answers of these questions will give us an understanding of the process as a whole, so we can proceed to model the major steps of the process in a high-level diagram.

This high-level diagram must fit on a single page.

From there, you can expand each activity of the high-level diagram into child-level diagrams, and then, adding only the amount of detail needed for your purpose.

Doing it the other way around (starting with more detailed activities) can get you a lot of unnecessary steps and details that might not even part of the process.

Let's see in more depth the core three steps to top-down modeling.

Step one: The high-level diagram

The high-level diagram just contains the major activities of the process. Ideally, it will fit on a single page and ten or fewer activities are enough. These activities are modeled as collapsed subprocesses.

We start by considering only the *happy path* first, using all kinds of activities, gateways and events to take the process from its initial to its end state.

Now we can add the exception/alternate paths. The end states of these paths are shown as separate end events in the high-level diagram.

You can use a specific type of start event to indicate how the process starts, for example, a timer start event to indicate that the process is scheduled or recurring.

You can add lanes in a top-level diagram, but only if it makes it more organized or easier to read.

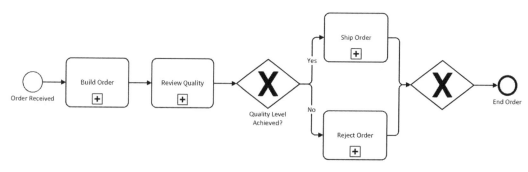

STEP TWO: THE CHILD-LEVEL DIAGRAMS

For each activity in the high-level diagram we create a child-level diagram to show its internal details. Each one is created as a separated diagram, linked to the high-level diagram.

The child-level diagrams should have a none start event. Their activities can also be collapsed subprocesses, which would be expanded in another layer of child-level diagrams.

You can use pools in these child-level diagrams. The only rule is that it has to be the same pool used (if any) in the parent-level diagram. You can also use lanes, but in contrast to pools, each child-level diagram can define its own lanes.

All the input or output flows to a subprocess in the high-level diagram, should be traceable to the child-level diagram. For example, if a subprocess is followed by a gateway, the subprocess should have as many end states as the gateway's branches and one of them should match the gateway label.

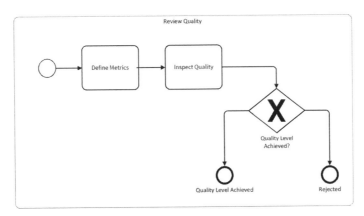

Step three: Adding detail

The key of this step is that you should only add **VALUABLE** information to a diagram.

But how do you know if something is valuable?

It has to be valuable in the **CONTEXT** of the business for the process and it must clarify or show how the process interacts with other entities.

Message flows for example, are not required by the BPMN specification. However, they provide information about interactions between participants, and that's make them valuable, so it is always recommended to draw them.

If something cannot be defined properly by using BPMN elements, use text annotations. In fact, you should always use text by labeling all the elements in your diagram. Use icons (in task types or event triggers) to make the logic clearer.

Finally, be consistent. If you use certain style to model, use it in all your diagrams. For example, if you model parallel flows using two or more sequence flows instead of using a parallel gateway, use them in all diagrams, not just a few. This would improve the communication, which is one of the main objectives of BPMN.

ONLY ADD VALUABLE INFORMATION TO A DIAGRAM

Chapter TEN

Appendix I
Diagram Summary

Process diagrams focus on the flow and sequence of a single business process.

Collaboration diagrams focus on the interaction (message exchange and its sequence) between participants.

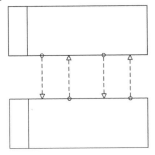

Conversation diagrams provide a general view of the interactions between participants.

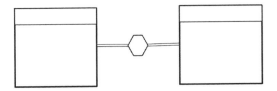

Choreography diagrams focus on how participants exchange messages to coordinate their interactions.

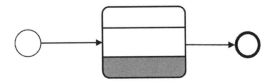

A process is the base of all modeling in BPMN. You start by describing the events and activities of the process in a single pool.

When you identify multiple participants in the process, you use a pool for each. In this case a collaboration diagram allows you to express interactions between participants in a higher level of abstraction than processes.

If there are a lot of message flows, you can group them into conversations. This add a higher layer of abstraction to express related messages in a simpler way.

Finally, in a choreography, we model a sequence of interactions between two or more participants. Nothing new is added to the context of the processes, it's just another view of the messages and their flow that can be also expressed as a conversation.

Appendix II

Events Summary

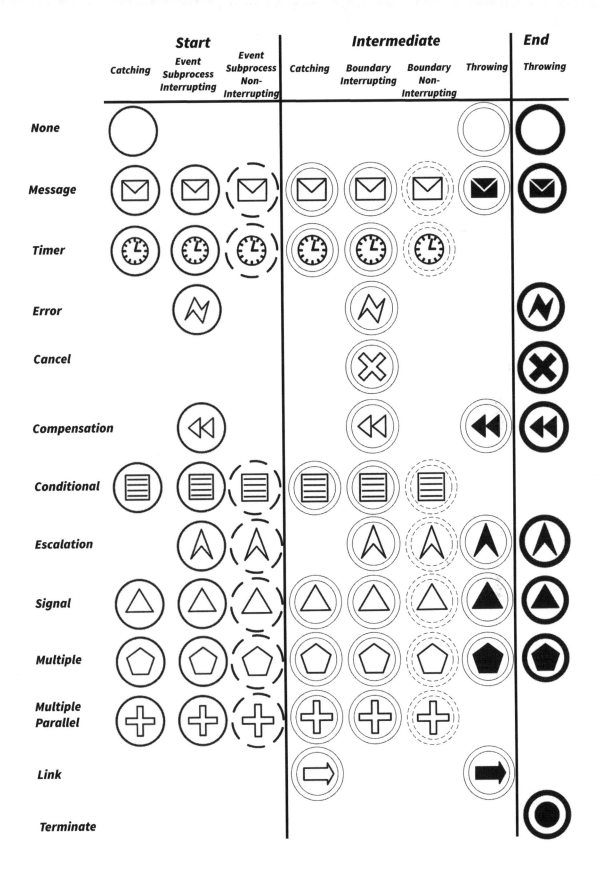

FINALLY

I hope you enjoyed this book. I tried to keep it as simple as possible and as the adage "An image is worth a thousand words" says, I also tried to fill it with images (most pages of the book have at least one image).

Anyway, feel free to contact me via Twitter (**@eh3rrera**) for any question, suggestion, or just about anything I can help you with.

Made in the USA
Middletown, DE
08 August 2015